Americanisms

The Illustrated Book of
Words Made in the USA

Edited and Compiled by
Gary Luke and Susan Quinn

SASQUATCH BOOKS
SEATTLE

Printed in Singapore
Published by Sasquatch Books
Distributed by Publishers Group West
09 08 07 06 05 04 03   6 5 4 3 2 1

Cover and interior design: Stewart A. Williams
Cover photograph: ©Bettmann/CORBIS
All interior photographs by Bettmann/CORBIS with the exception of "Showgirls Receive Influenza Injections" and "Frank Zappa" by Hulton-Deutsch Collection/CORBIS and "Meter Maid Places Ticket on Windshield" by Jack Moebes/CORBIS
Copy editor: Sherri Schultz

Library of Congress Cataloging-in-Publication Data
Luke, Gary, 1954-
     Americanism: some words of our own / Gary Luke and Susan Quinn.
          p. cm.
     ISBN: 1-57061-385-0
     1. Americanism–Dictionaries. 2. English language–United States–Dictionaries.
     I. Quinn, Susan R. II. Title.

     PE2835.L85 2003
     423.1–dc21   2002044648

Sasquatch Books
119 South Main Street, Suite 400
Seattle, Washington 98104
206-467-4300
www.sasquatchbooks.com
books@sasquatchbooks.com

Introduction

Full disclosure has become fashionable lately, so here's ours. We are not scholars or etymologists. We are authors in only the loosest sense of the word. "Compilers" might be the most appropriate moniker. But we are book people, and we have long wanted to find a book like the one you are holding. Finally, we wrote it ourselves.

By "Americanisms," we mean words that have been coined or adopted in the United States and are now part of the English language. Consider such commonplace words as hamburger, motel, and popcorn; all are Americanisms.

Compiling this book was a sort of patriotic act for us. Some Americans display their sentiments by mounting a standard atop the roof rack of the family Subaru and unfurling Old Glory for a trip to the grocery store, and there's nothing wrong with that. But it's not the only way to be a patriot. Exploring the rich and sometimes surprising universe of the dictionary to unearth Americanisms made us exclaim more than a few times, "Bodacious beauty parlors! Is that really an Americanism?"

Many words reflect the importance of business and enterprise in the American experience: cash register, typewriter, paycheck, salesperson. The nation's far-reaching roots brought such words as lasso, chutzpah, Nisei, Afro, and, of course, acculturate and multiculturalism. We also dredged up some words from the recent past that are nearing disuse: hula hoop, muumuu, neck (the thing you used to do on dates), beauty parlor. And then there were the words that ought to be printed in some stars-and-stripes font: baseball, intestinal fortitude, rodeo, shotgun, and RV.

Language, as you will recall from that obligatory college lecture, is dynamic. The high-tech world probably introduces or makes obsolete a new word every day (whither floppy disk?). We make no claims of completeness or currency; this little book is no dictionary. And the photos are just the kind of interpretive images that no self-respecting dictionary editor would ever allow.

—G. L. and S. Q.

noun: a devastating bomb whose power is derived from nuclear fission; one of the "weapons of mass destruction." Also atomic bomb.

a-bomb

"We thank God the atomic bomb came to us instead of to our enemies and we pray that God may guide us to use it in His ways and for His purposes."

—President Harry S. Truman

verb: to adapt in order to be more like a surrounding or coveted culture.

acculturate

Marilyn and Bill sought to acculturate themselves to sunny old Mexico by buying and donning sombreros as soon as they landed in Acapulco. They felt like natives. They looked like pale Americans from Canton, Ohio, with ridiculous hats on.

noun: a tight and curly hairstyle
made popular in the 1960s
by African Americans.

afro

"Shaft wore one, and so did Black Panther
leader Angela Davis. As black pride took
to the streets, African Americans not only
reclaimed an affection for African dress and
accessories, but many stopped processing and
relaxing their hair in an attempt to conform
to white standards of beauty. They shouted
'Black Is Beautiful' and let the natural kinky state
grow into a hair halo called the Afro."

—yesterdayland.com

noun: the conglomerate industry made up of all aspects of the farming business—production, growing, machinery, and so on.

agribusiness

"Fresno profited from irrigated farming in the 1880s. Due to the extensive and sophisticated agribusiness in the valley, the city dramatically expanded, becoming one of the fastest-growing cities in the U.S."

—*Columbia Gazeteer, 2001*

interj.: used in Hawaii and by poseurs nationwide, a greeting meaning both hello and goodbye.

aloha

"Aloha `oe, aloha `oe
E ke onaona noho i ka lipo. One fond embrace,
A ho`i a`e au. Until we meet again . . . "

—Queen Lili`uokalani

adj.: of or relating to the era prior to the Civil War.

antebellum

"There's a couch Sherman slept on in
Sandersville during his 'March to the Sea,' there
are bloodstains on the floor of a church used
as a hospital in Ringgold, there are bullet holes
in the siding of an antebellum home
at Barnsley Gardens. . . ."

—*The Civil War in Georgia: An Illustrated Travelers Guide*

noun: a substance made up of microorganisms and/or fungi, often used to treat the spread of infections and infectious diseases.

antibiotic

"The greatest analgesic, soporific, stimulant, tranquilizer, narcotic, and to some extent even antibiotic—in short, the closest thing to a genuine panacea—known to medical science is work."

—Thomas Szasz, psychoanalyst

noun: one who takes on the responsibility of watching over children in the temporary absence of parents and/or guardians; one who has to constantly watch over a process or organization.

babysitter

"When babysitting, NEVER

• Open the door to anyone before checking to see who it is.

• Open the door to strangers, including delivery people.

• Let anyone inside, including people you know, if they are using alcohol, drugs, or acting weird.

• Tell a stranger on the phone that you are the babysitter.

• Invite your friends over to visit.

• Stay anywhere you feel unsafe, smell smoke, or hear a fire or smoke alarm.

• Go outside to check on something strange, such as an unusual noise."

—*American Red Cross Babysitter's Handbook*

plural noun: a place located far from any urban center and often considered culturally retarded.

backwoods

"You think I'd talk to a dog? Do you think I'd ask a dog whether you are good or evil? Do you think I'm some sort of backwoods weirdo with a barn full of skulls and knives I sharpen every day in anticipation for Armageddon?"

—Tod in *A Life Less Ordinary*

noun: a place, often a large stadium,
where ballgames are played.

ballpark

"The most beautiful thing in the world
is a ballpark filled with people."

—Bill Veeck, baseball executive

plural noun: a portion of hair that is cut across the forehead and above the eyebrows and, more often than not, straight and blunt.

bangs

"The resemblance between Louise and me started with our measurements; at a height of four feet eleven inches, we each weighed a meager ninety-two pounds; and, in a world where it was almost an obligation to be blond, we never tampered with the blue-black color of our hair. We wore it at shoulder length and were the first of the trend-setters to venture into bangs."

—Anita Loos

noun: a four- to five-stringed instrument consisting of a long narrow neck and a circular body. Often played in bluegrass music.

banjo

"We pretty much defined our music as 'mountain music.' I was always around bluegrass music. I especially loved the banjo. An old man that used to live up the road from us showed me how to play. And actually, if I don't have these long fingernails on I can still play in that old 'clawhammer' style."

—Dolly Parton

noun: a game played by children and millionaires involving a leather-covered ball and a wooden bat, either on a field or in a zillion-dollar stadium, with a circuit of four bases. Also, the ball used in the aforementioned game.

baseball

"Baseball is 90 percent mental. The other half is physical."

—Yogi Berra

noun: a follower of the Beat generation. Often characterized by style of dress and speech patterns (e.g., "Hey, daddy-o"). From Beat generation + nik.

beatnik

"It is not my fault that certain so-called bohemian elements have found in my writings something to hang their peculiar beatnik theories on."

—Jack Kerouac

noun: a retail establishment offering services including washing, cutting, and styling hair; it may also provide cosmetic care of hands and complexion.

beauty parlor

"Seymour finally called me for a date, and I went immediately to the beauty parlor."

—Auntie Verlinda

noun: a post–World War II style of jazz characterized by complex rhythms and harmonies and improvisations by solo performers—often regarded as brilliant. Performers associated with the style include Charlie Parker, Dizzy Gillespie, Sarah Vaughan, and Thelonious Monk.

bebop

"From the beginning of her career Vaughan's range and versatility as a singer were clearly evident. A bebop jazz devotee, only Ella Fitzgerald could scat with greater expertise."

—Oreen Scott

bermuda shorts

"They used to have a fish on the menu . . . that was smoked, grilled and peppered. . . . They did everything to this fish but pistol-whip it and dress it in Bermuda shorts."

—William E. Geist, author of *Little League Confidential*

noun: another name for the New York Stock Exchange, derived from the large electronic board showing stock activity.

big board

"The decline is the third consecutive drop in the price of a seat on the exchange, the nation's biggest. In October, the price fell 8 percent. Exchange seats had gained in value over the last several years as average daily trading on the Big Board has climbed. In June, the price rose 2 percent."

—*Bloomberg News*

noun: a gambling game of chance involving randomly chosen numbers and letters, in which players mark the matches on their scorecards.

bingo

"The religion of Christ is not aspirin to deaden the pain of living, it is not a discussion group, nor a miraculous medal nor a piety, nor bingo for God."

—John Monaghan, Roman Catholic priest

noun: contraception; the planning and intentional
regulation of pregnancy by use of contraception.

birth control

"If men got pregnant, there would
be safe, reliable methods of birth control.
They'd be inexpensive, too."

—Anna Quindlen, author of *Black and Blue*

noun: a movement among African Americans in the 1960s declaring the black community's intention and need to determine its destiny by any means necessary.

black power

"The essay tells the chilling story of a half-black Trinidadian named Michael Malik (or Michael X), who started out as a pimp and drug pusher, became the darling of white radicals in London and returned to Trinidad in 1971 as an avatar of Black Power; he would end up being hanged in 1975, after orchestrating the murders of two followers."

—Michiko Kakutani, *The New York Times*

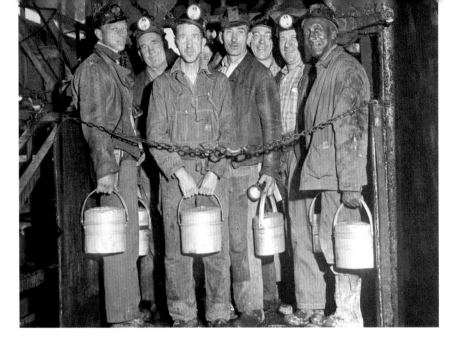

adj.: pertaining to industrial workers and laborers;
originally from the blue chambray cloth of their shirts.

blue-collar

"In some [Russian] circles Stalin has in fact been making
a comeback. His portrait hangs above the dashboard of trucks, a
symbol of blue-collar nostalgia for a tough leader."

—Serge Schmemann, author of *Soviets*

noun: leader; one who is in charge and in command.

boss

"When I first heard Elvis's voice I just knew that I wasn't going to work for anybody and nobody was gonna be my boss. Hearing him for the first time was like busting out of jail."

—Bob Dylan

noun: miser; one who is notoriously stingy with money.

cheapskate

"The most plausible theory about the 'skate' in 'cheapskate' traces it to the Scots word 'skate,' a term of contempt which apparently also crops up in a slightly different form in the archaic term 'blatherskite,' meaning a person who blathers, or babbles nonsense. If this theory is true, 'cheapskate' would thus translate as essentially 'stingy creep,' which makes sense."

—Evan Morris, *The Word Detective*

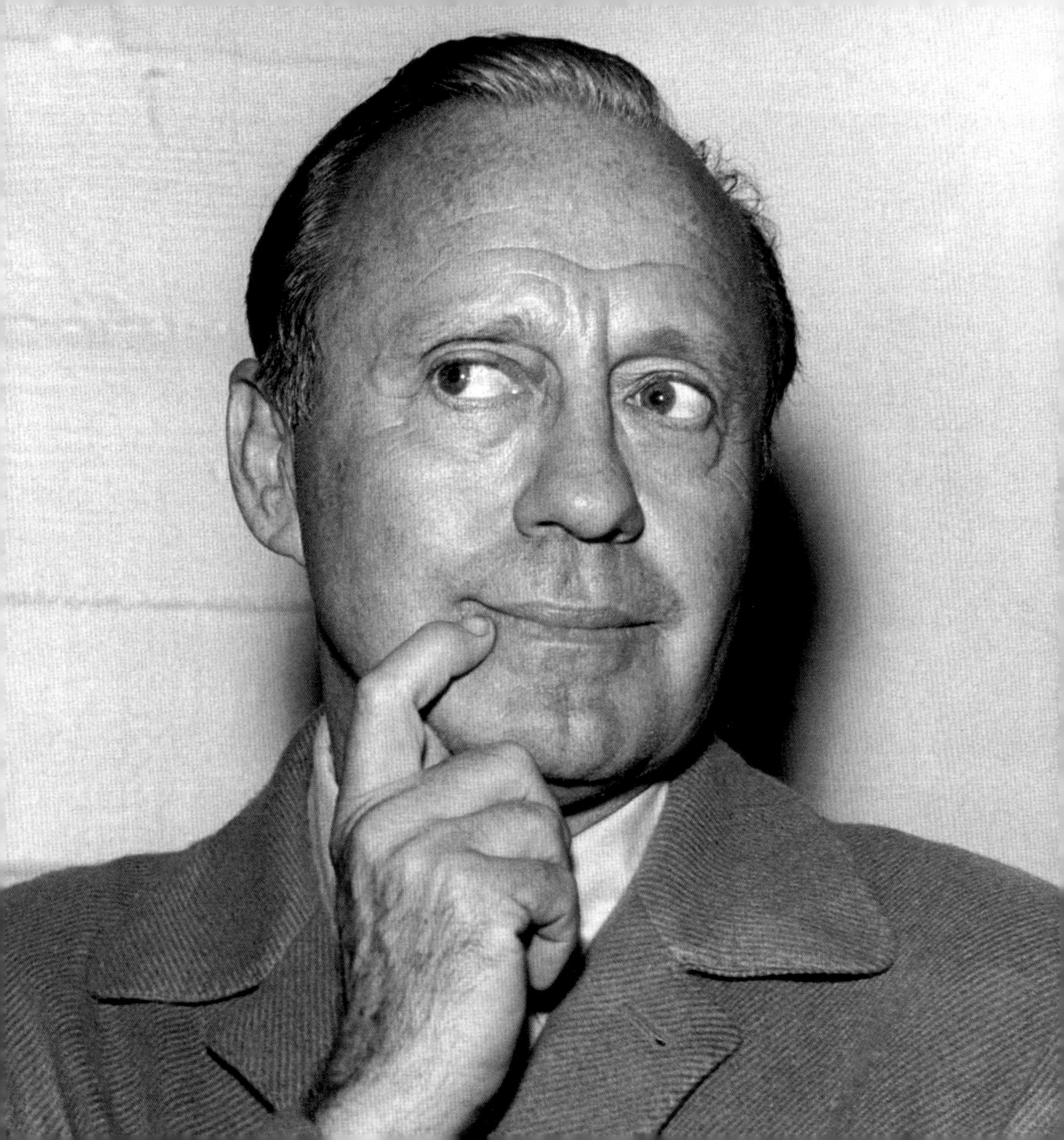

noun: a display of nerves, gusto and, most importantly, in the eyes of the observer, unmitigated gall. Derived from the Yiddish *khutspe.*

chutzpah

"Viva chutzpah!"

—Senator Joe Leiberman in Los Angeles

noun: a volume of recipes.

cookbook

"The argument that making contraceptives available to young people would prevent teen pregnancies is ridiculous. That's like offering a cookbook as a cure to people who are trying to lose weight."

—Jerry Falwell

noun: one who makes a living by dishonest methods.

crook

"People have got to know whether or not their president is a crook. Well, I'm not a crook."

—Richard M. Nixon

noun: one who abandons something before it is finished—especially school.

dropout

"My advice to people today is as follows: If you take the game of life seriously, if you take your nervous system seriously, if you take your sense organs seriously, if you take the energy process seriously, you must turn on, tune in, and drop out."

—Timothy Leary

noun: one who regularly drinks excessive amounts of alcohol; an alcoholic.

adj.: intoxicated; physically or mentally affected by alcohol consumption.

drunk

"Alcohol removes inhibitions—like that scared little mouse who got drunk and shook his whiskers and shouted: 'Now bring on that damn cat!'"

—Eleanor Early

interj.: an expression of exasperation in response to banality or stupidity.

duh

"According to New York publishers, Bill Clinton will get more money for his book than Hillary Clinton got for hers. Well, duh. At least his book has some sex in it."

—Jay Leno

verb: to kill with electricity; to execute a person by such means.

electrocute

"I would like to electrocute everyone who uses the word 'fair' in connection with income tax policies."

—*William F. Buckley*

noun: a small beard on the chin, styled into a point, said to resemble the beard of a billy goat —thus, goatee.

goatee

An old Massachusetts ordinance declares goatees illegal unless you first pay a special license fee for the privilege of wearing one in public. We wish that law had stayed in effect through the 1990s dot-com goatee madness.

noun: a large, round semitropical citrus fruit with a yellow rind and a pink or whitish juicy interior; probably so called because the fruit grows in clusters.

grapefruit

"If the Americans, in addition to the eagle and the Stars and Stripes and the more unofficial symbols of bison, moose, and Indian, should ever need another emblem, one which is friendly and pleasant, then I think they should choose the grapefruit. Or rather the half grapefruit, for this fruit only comes in halves, I believe. Practically speaking, it is always yellow, always just as fresh and well served. And it always comes at the same, still hopeful hour of the morning."

—Johan Huizinga, cultural historian

noun: a thong panty consisting of a small triangular piece of fabric supported by two elastic straps. Attributed to strippers circa 1936–perhaps short for "girdle string."

g-string

"As a model she was fearless; there was nothing she wouldn't do for a picture. Photographer Peter Beard once had her scale a bask of sleepy crocodiles in her G-string."

—George Epaminondas, about Janice Dickinson

noun: a person of mixed racial descent, especially a person of Native American and white parentage.

half-breed

"Half-breed, that's all I ever heard. Half-breed, how I learned to hate the word."

—Cher

noun: a sandwich made of a grilled ground beef patty served between the two halves of a baked bun.

hamburger

"To think that between a Hamburger and a Humburger, she would—invariably, with icy precision—plump for the former."

—Vladimir Nabokov, Lolita

noun: originally, the young people in the 1960s who rejected conventional society in favor of drugs, communal living, and mystical or natural lifestyles.

hippie

"The Internet is an important cultural phenomenon, but that doesn't excuse its failure to comply with basic economic laws. The problem is that it was devised by a bunch of hippie anarchists."

—Thomas Nolle

noun: a surfer.

hodad

"A 'hodad' is a person who never goes in the water but acts and dresses as if he does. A 'brodad' is a 'hodad' who further irritates surfers by calling everyone 'bro'— including his mom."

—Trevor "Coconut" Cralle,
aka the Shakespeare of Surf

noun: a stoppage; the act of halting and robbing.

holdup

"By the age of six the average child will have completed the basic American education. . . . From television, the child will have learned how to pick a lock, commit a fairly elaborate bank holdup, prevent wetness all day long, get the laundry twice as white, and kill people with a variety of sophisticated armaments."

—Russell Baker, author of *Growing Up*

noun: in baseball, the event in which the batter hits the ball such that she or he can run the entire circuit of three bases and home plate.

home run

"After I hit a home run I had a habit of running the bases with my head down. I figured the pitcher already felt bad enough without me showing him up rounding the bases."

—Mickey Mantle

noun: the trademarked name for a plastic hoop that is twirled around the torso for play and exercise.

hula hoop

"The HULA HOOP® Original comes in three swirly colors and three hoop sizes. How many Hoops can you keep going at once?"

—Wham-O, Inc.

noun: endurance and courage; aka guts.

intestinal fortitude

"Kudos to the protesters. I wish I had the intestinal fortitude to stand with them and face the technocrats, the bureaucrats, the corpo-rats, scheming to make zillions at the cost of fellow billions."

—Slate.com reader on protests of the World Trade Organization

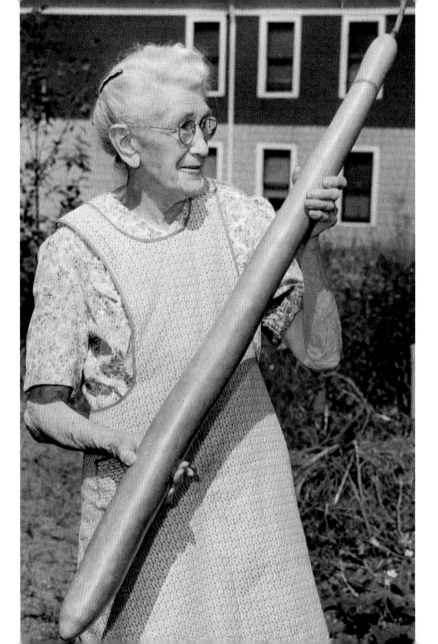

adj.: extremely oversized.

jumbo

"Jumbo Jellyfish Bedeviling
Local Fishermen Matsue
(Kyodo)—Fishermen along the
Sea of Japan coast, especially
those near Shimane and Fukui
prefectures, have been plagued
by giant jellyfish since August."

—*Japan Times*

noun: a rope or length of hide with a sliding noose at one end that is used to catch cattle or horses. Likely derived from the Spanish *lazo. verb:* to capture an animal or other object with a lasso.

lasso

The Texas Skip is that little routine of spinning a large vertical loop with a lasso, then hopping through it while the lasso is in motion. Yippee-ti-yi-yo!

noun: the customary behavior and values of a group or individual.

lifestyle

"I've been trying for some time to develop a lifestyle that doesn't require my presence."

—Gary Trudeau

noun: a person employed to deliver mail.

mailman

"I would especially like to recourt the Muse of poetry, who ran off with the mailman four years ago, and drops me only a scribbled postcard from time to time."

—John Updike

noun: a person employed to write and disseminate notices of parking violations. Once a primarily female occupation, thus maid.

meter maid

"Lovely Rita, meter maid, nothing can come between us. When it gets dark I tow your heart away."

—The Beatles, "Lovely Rita"

noun: To walk on the surface of the moon, inspired by *Apollo 11*'s landing of the first man on the moon in 1969. Subsequent expeditions brought us "moon golf" and "moon drives."

moonwalk

"That's one small step for man,
one giant leap for mankind."

—Neil Armstrong, immediately following
the very first moonwalk

noun: an amphibian old or slow enough to grow green algae on its back; a very conservative or old-fashioned person.

mossback

". . . I realized that no matter what happens, I'm here to stay. A Seattle native, born and bred. A mossback with no intention of moving anywhere else."

—Knute Berger, editor, *Seattle Weekly*

noun: a lodging establishment, often described by the adjective "seedy," that furnishes free parking, cable TV, and the occasional "magic fingers massage" mechanism in the bed. Motor + hotel = motel.

motel

"The hotel was once where things coalesced, where you could meet both townspeople and travelers. Not so in a motel. No matter how you build it, the motel remains the haunt of the quick and dirty, where the only locals are Chamber of Commerce boys every fourth Thursday. Who ever heard the returning traveler exclaim over one of the great motels of the world he stayed in? Motels can be big, but never grand."

—William Least Heat-Moon, author of *Blue Highways*

noun: a procession of automobiles.
The word is a combination of
motor + cavalcade.

motorcade

"Public figures such as royalty,
presidents, and rock bands often
travel via motorcade, but this
particular mode of getting
from here to there may draw
the attention of assassins,
gunmen, demonstrators, and
other ill-wishers."

—Jaffy Ryder

noun: a technology that creates the illusion of a moving picture via rapidly changing still photographs.

movie

"In a novel a hero can lay ten girls and marry a virgin for a finish. In a movie this is not allowed. The hero, as well as the heroine, has to be a virgin. The villain can lay anybody he wants, have as much fun as he wants cheating and stealing, getting rich and whipping the servants. But you have to shoot him in the end."

—Herbert Mankiewicz, U.S. journalist and screenwriter

adj.: concerning several cultures; relating to an educational theory that teaches about many cultures, not solely the dominant one.

multicultural

"The American cause the GIs in Normandy gave their lives to achieve had real character. Their cause was liberty, not multiculturalism."

—Kim Holmes, Ph.D., Heritage Lecture #671

noun: a mixed-breed dog; mongrel.

mutt

"A weimaraner bore a sign that read 'Congress Don't Roll Over / You'll Have to Scoop Up After Bush.' A Jack Russell terrier wore a T-shirt scrawled with the simple statement 'No War!' And Max, a tiny 10-year-old mutt, wore a red sweater emblazoned with a slogan involving Bush and nature that was blunt, if not a little crude."

—*Seattle Times*

noun: A long, loose style of dress that originated in Hawaii.

muumuu

"Hawaiian muumuu made in Honolulu, Hawaii, by Lisa Maru Design Creations. Size 3X. Very pretty muumuu! This muumuu would be wonderful for that summer luau, ocean cruise, or party. It has a flare line for a slimming effect and oversized raglan sleeves. Color is soft blue with floral design on skirt and yoke with pink trim. Worn just a couple of times. No stains or holes."

—Seller's posting on eBay

noun: one who busts a drug user or dealer, often by operating undercover; tattletale. Short for narcotics officer.

narc

"Attention, workplace drug abusers. That friendly colleague who may clock in with you, clock out with you, party with you, and even ask to buy some of your personal stash of weed may not be a friend at all. She may be a narc for hire."

—Steve Young, *The Tennessean*

noun: kissing, caressing, making out,
petting, fondling, and so on.

necking

"Whoever named it necking
was a poor judge of anatomy."
—Groucho Marx

noun: a person born in the United States of parents who emigrated from Japan; from the Japanese words for "second generation."

nisei

"Pound for pound, the nisei players were as good as the Major Leaguers. They ate, thought, and slept the game."

—Al Beir, batboy for Babe Ruth and Lou Gehrig

adv., adj., interj.: all right or correct. Also O.K., okay. Possibly an abbreviation for the nineteenth-century slang term *oll korrect.*

ok

"One out of four people in this country is mentally unbalanced. Think of your three closest friends; if they seem OK, then you're the one."

—Ann Landers

noun: an art movement of the 1960s characterized by the use of optical illusions.

op art

"In the 1960s, the term 'Op Art' was coined to describe the work of a growing group of abstract painters. This movement was led by Vasarely and Bridget Riley. Other Op Artists included Richard Anuszkiewicz, Jesús-Rafael Soto, Kenneth Noland, François Morellet, and Lawrence Poons."

—*Artcyclopedia*

noun: a check received for wages or salary.

paycheck

"For a lot of people, the weekly paycheck is 'take-home pay' because home is the only place they can afford to go with it."

—Charles A. Jaffe,
The Boston Globe columnist

noun: pants that hit between the ankle and knee, originally created to make bicycle riding easier for women. Popular in the 1940s and '50s.

pedal pusher

"Capris, pedal pushers, clam diggers, flood pants—call them what you will—the three-quarter-length trousers are crossing gender boundaries. At least, that's what some ready-to-wear houses—Perry Ellis, BCBG and others—would like us to think, as they crop their pants for men and try to get guys to wear them. 'I think in the summer it's adorable,' one woman says, 'if they have cute ankles.'"

—*CNN*

noun: any doctrine maintaining that spiritual, personal, or social perfection is possible; a personal ethos of perfection.

perfectionism

"Perfectionism refers to a set of self-defeating thoughts and behaviors aimed at reaching excessively high and unrealistic goals. Perfectionism is often mistakenly seen in our society as desirable or even necessary for success. However, recent studies have shown that perfectionistic attitudes actually interfere with success."

—State University of New York
Potsdam Counseling Center

adj.: fake or make-believe.

phony

"Strip away the phony tinsel of Hollywood and you find the real tinsel underneath."

—Oscar Levant, composer, pianist, actor

noun: typically, a round, flat bread topped with tomato sauce, cheese, and sometimes sausage and other items. Probably a substitution of the Italian pizza, meaning point or edge, for the Greek pitta, bread.

pizza

"Imagine if all of life were determined by majority rule. Every meal would be a pizza. Every pair of pants, even those in a Brooks Brothers suit, would be stonewashed denim."

—P. J. O'Rourke

noun: ongoing live commentary broadcasting the actions and details of a sport or event.

play-by-play

"His [radio-announcer] tryout consisted of making up a play-by-play broadcast for an imaginary football game. He did well enough, and he was signed on."

—*Grolier Encyclopedia entry for Ronald Reagan*

noun: traditionally a form of gambling played with playing cards, the object of which is to collect cards in successively better combinations.

poker

"The poker player learns that sometimes both science and common sense are wrong; that the bumblebee can fly; that, perhaps, one should never trust an expert; that there are more things in heaven and earth than are dreamt of by those with an academic bent."

—David Mamet

noun: a derivative of corn, specially grown to explode at high
temperatures; a favorite of moviegoers.

popcorn

"In American Indian folklore, some tribes were
said to believe that quiet, contented spirits lived
inside of each popcorn kernel. When their houses
were heated, the spirits would become angrier
and angrier, shaking the kernels, and when the
heat became unbearable, they would burst out of
their homes and into the air in a disgruntled puff
of steam."

—Linda Stradley, author of
I'll Have What They're Having: Legendary Local Cuisine

noun: a formal dance.
Short for promenade.

prom

"And there was that wholesale libel on a Yale prom: If all the girls attending it were laid end to end, Mrs. Parker said, she wouldn't be at all surprised."

—*Alexander Woollcott on Dorothy Parker*

noun: anything performed or made speedily.

adj.: having the qualities of rapidity.

quickie

"If you're turned on at an inopportune time, act on your feelings. Although it feels a little bit naughty, a quickie will help you stay faithful."

—*Cosmopolitan*

plural noun: an early indoor TV antenna that was situated on the back or top of the television. Two antennae are moved around to receive optimum reception; or exceptionally keen hearing

rabbit ears

"... he was a terrific umpire, although he had one of the worst cases of rabbit ears I've ever seen."

—Whitey Herzog

noun: a semisynthetic fabric made from wood pulp, wool felt, and synthetic fluids.

rayon

"Of all the fibers, rayon is probably the most perplexing to consumers. It can be found in cotton-like end uses, as well as sumptuous velvets and taffetas. It may function successfully in absorbent hygiene and incontinence pads and equally well providing strength in tire cords. What is this fiber that has so many faces?"

—Joyce A. Smith, Ph.D., Ohio State University Extension
Specialist, Apparel and Textiles

noun: a room where one engages in recreational activities such as playing games, watching television, and exercising.

rec room

"The atmosphere in the Grand Avenue building is as far from a prison as imaginable. Everything is carpeted. A rec room has an elaborate weight-training machine and a pool table any residential college could be proud of. Offenders—'clients,' as they're known here—walk around freely. There are no guns, no bars."

—Joshua Benton, *The Yale Herald*

noun: a public competition involving cowboy skills. Derived from the Spanish *rodear,* to go around.

rodeo

"After an hour of civilized conversation about French paintings, the European Common Market, and the condition of the rodeo arena in Ponoka, Don invited his date to go with him to check the cows."

—Baxter Black, cowboy poet and humorist

noun: an amusement park ride involving a railway with dramatic climbs and drops.

adj.: characterized by ups and downs.

roller coaster

"It was in 1927 that the benchmark for roller coasters was built. Called the Cyclone, and built at Coney Island, it featured an 85-foot plunge and incredible 60-degree angles. Today, the Cyclone is still an industry standard."

—International Association of Amusement Parks and Attractions

noun: a candidate for the lesser of two associated elected offices; a horse that sets the pace for another in a race.

running mate

"When George W. Bush introduced his running mate, his father's former Defense Secretary Dick Cheney, and they stood Tuesday afternoon before a row of American flags, the Bush camp finally got what it wanted: an image to banish the family's disastrous 1988 'mystery date' moment, when J. Danforth Quayle, he of the infamous deer-in-the-headlights demeanor, joined the last Bush ticket, and kept late-night comedians in punch lines for the next 12 years."

—Joan Walsh, News Editor, *Salon.com*

noun: a long, raised walkway, with seats below on either side, utilized by beauty pageant contestants, models, and others to display their wares; a long strip used by airplanes to take off and land.

runway

"Contestants will be judged on the quality and professionalism of their costumes, make-up and modeling. . . . Contestants will be asked to walk a runway in their Klingon persona. Poise, grace and the authenticity of their persona will be the criteria for judging."

—2002 Miss Klingon Empire Beauty Pageant

noun: recreational vehicle.

RV

"To the tent people, RV campers are impostors, lazy despoilers of the wilderness, supersized, expecting the outdoors to accommodate them, instead of giving in to nature's bedroom. . . . To the RV people, tent campers are slackers, not particularly fresh-smelling, even a little suspect."

—*The New York Times*

noun: a large upright cactus with vertical branches from the main stem that grow up to 60 feet tall and bear white flowers.

saguaro

"The saguaro doom story [that the cactus is disappearing] first surfaced in the 1940s; at that time little was known about saguaro ecology."

—Arizona-Sonora Desert Museum

noun: one whose job it is to sell goods or services.

salesperson

Q. What's the difference between a used-car
dealer and a computer salesman?
A. The used-car dealer knows he's lying.

—Popular riddle among computer nerds

noun: a rascal; a native white Southerner who cooperated with occupying officials during Reconstruction.

scalawag

"The South Was Right! should be in every Southern home at the right hand of everyone who ever has or ever will have to argue with a Carpetbagger, Scalawag, or Radical."

—*Southern Patriot*

[From the Independent Monitor, Tuscaloosa, Alabama, September 1, 1868.]

A PROSPECTIVE SCENE IN THE CITY OF OAKS, 4TH OF MARCH, 1869.

"Hang, curs, hang! * * * * * *Their* complexion is perfect gallows. Stand fast, good fate, to *their* hanging! * * * * * If they be not born to be hanged, our case is miserable."

The above cut represents the fate in store for those great pests of Southern society—the carpet-bagger and scalawag—if found in Dixie's land after the break of day on the 4th of March next.

A Facsimile put in Evidence before the Congressional Committee.

noun: a coquettish young woman.

sex kitten

"You know, a lot of people assumed you were hired because you were a blond, Republican sex kitten. They were obviously wrong."

—White House staffer on *The West Wing*

"We've seen what transpired in England, when police went down the registration list and called in all privately owned guns. It's not a pretty sight, if fine firearms stir fond memories. Beautifully crafted shotguns, World War I heirlooms, family keepsakes. All went into the pile to be pulverized like rubbish and hauled away as so much scrap metal."

—Charlton Heston

noun: a smoothbore gun used to fire small shot at short range to hunt small game. *adverb:* to sit atop a stagecoach bearing arms as a guard, as in "to ride shotgun."

shotgun

noun: movies, television, the stage, and even the circus, when considered as an industry (rather than as art and culture).

show business

"Politics is just like show business: You have a hell of an opening, coast for a while, and then have a hell of a close."

—Ronald Reagan

noun: a plainclothes federal agent stationed aboard airliners
to prevent skyjacking or other crimes.

sky marshal

"Why do they insist on sky marshals, an
expensive alternative that can actually increase
risk, given that a marshal can be relieved of his
or her weapon by the hijackers, who then have
the only arms on the plane?"

—James V. DeLong, arguing for arming airline employees

noun: a confused or nonfunctional situation. A World War II military acronym for "situation normal, all fucked up."

snafu

"In the elections business, when there's a snafu, the powers that be start paying attention. Then you can get the money you need."

—Bob Terwilliger, auditor for
Snohomish County, Washington

noun: a comfortable shoe with a cloth upper and a rubber sole.

sneaker

"More than 200 dot-coms have already gone sneakers-up. . . "

—Roger McNamee, general partner at venture capital firm Integral Capital Partners

noun: a significant person in fashionable society, e.g., a rich person among the wealthy.

socialite

"Socialite women meet socialite men and mate and breed socialite children so that we can fund small opera companies and ballet troupes because there is no government subsidy."

—Sugar Rautbord, Chicago socialite and novelist

noun: a popular style of music developed in the 1950s and later by African Americans, considered a secular form of gospel music.

soul music

"Worse yet, after a glorious two-decade reign as the East Coast capital of soul music, Philly has produced little in the way of lasting musical value."

—*Rolling Stone*

noun: a sudden headlong rush of frenzied creatures, usually cattle, horses, or shoppers. Also the name of a Western gathering of people involving a celebration, a rodeo, and exhibits. *verb:* to move in or be part of a stampede.

stampede

"During the cattle drives, Texas cowboy music came into national significance. Its practical purpose is well known—it was used primarily to keep the herds quiet atnight, for often a ballad sung loudly and continuously enough might prevent a stampede."

—*WPA Guide to Texas*

noun: ice cream served with syrup and frequently nuts, whipped cream, and cherries; possibly a deliberate alternate spelling of Sunday.

sundae

"Thin people turn surly, mean, and hard at a young age because they never learn the value of a hot fudge sundae for easing tension. Thin people don't like gooey soft things because they themselves are neither gooey nor soft. They are crunchy and dull, like carrots. They go straight to the heart of the matter while fat people let things stay all blurry and hazy and vague, the way things actually are." —Suzanne Britt, U.S. columnist

adj.: not tasteful; shabby; showy or gaudy.

tacky

"Kitchens were different then, too—not only what came out of them, but their smells and sounds. A hot pie cooling smells different from a frozen pie thawing. Oilcloth and linoleum and apples in an open bowl and ruffled rubber aprons make a different aromatic mix from Formica and ceramic tile and mangoes in an acrylic fruit ripener and plastic-coated aprons printed with 'Who invited all these tacky people?'"

—Peg Bracken, author of *The I Hate to Cook Book*

noun: an informer, especially among children.

tattletale

"CYBERsitter is in one way the strictest of the programs: It's a tattletale. The software keeps a log of the sites the child has attempted to access, 'including attempts to access blocked material.'"

—*Slate.com*

noun: a person in his or her teens. This age group has been called teeners, adolescents, and just plain impossible.

teenager

"Remember that as a teenager you are at the last stage in your life when you will be happy to hear that the phone is for you."

—Fran Lebowitz, author of *Metropolitan Life*

noun: an American Indian conical tent constructed with long poles and, frequently, animal skins. From the Dakota Sioux words for "used to live in." Also spelled teepee, tipi.

tepee

"Out of the cave, the tribal tepee, the pueblo, the community fortress, man emerged to build himself a house of his own with a shelter in it for himself and his diversions. Every age has seen it so."

—Phyllis McGinley, *A Lost Privilege*

noun: a handmade axlike weapon used by Native Americans for both defense and offense.

tomahawk

"I hope we shall give them a thorough drubbing this summer, and then change our tomahawk into a golden chain of friendship."

—Thomas Jefferson

noun: a writing machine that produces letters replicating typesetting.

typewriter

"I get up in the morning, torture a typewriter until it screams, then stop."
—Clarence B. Kelland

plural noun: underwear, or undergarment, worn on the lower half of the body.

underpants

". . . take all the kings and their cabinets and their generals, put 'em in the center dressed in their underpants, and let them fight it out with clubs. The best country wins."

—Maxwell Anderson, U.S. playwright

noun: a small mechanical device whose name often cannot be recalled. Likely derived from gadget.

widget

"Forget whether or not the widget works. It's how decent you are when it doesn't that really counts. Got that, techies?"

—Tom Peters, business guru

noun: a number too large to count.

adj.: of or amounting to a zillion

zillion

"I'm in a business where the odds of ever earning a living are a zillion to one, so I know it can be done."

—Marcia Wallace, actress

Low-down on the Photos

A-bomb *Atomic cloud over Bikini Atoll* • **Acculturate** *Japanese children* • **Afro** *Albino man with Afro* • **Agribusiness** *Skip-row planting in Tennessee* • **Aloha** *Ronald and Nancy Reagan* • **Antebellub** *Vivien Leigh in* Gone with the Wind • **Antibiotic** *Showgirls receive flu injections* • **Babysitter** *The children's playroom at Marshall Field's department store* • **Backwoods** *Actor Burt Reynolds in* Deliverance • **Ballpark** *Joe DiMaggio at Old Timers Day, 1963* • **Bangs** *Louise Brooks* • **Banjo** *Dolly Parton in concert* • **Baseball** *Pitcher Carl Hubbell* • **Beatnik** *Author Jack Kerouac* • **Beauty parlor** *Ladies at a beauty parlor in Boston* • **Bebop** *Sarah Vaughan* • **Bermuda shorts** *President Eisenhower with Sherman Adams* • **Big Board** *The New York Stock Exchange* • **Bingo** *New Jersey Bingo winner* • **Birth control** *Family planning poster* • **Black Power** *Yale cheerleaders give Black Power salute* • **Blue-collar** *Pennsylvania miner* • **Boss** *Gangster Sam Giancana* • **Cheapskate** *Jack Benny* • **Chutzpah** *Rosa Parks on the bus, 1956* • **Cookbook** *Julia Child* • **Crook** *Richard Nixon in Savannah* • **Dropout** *Dr. Timothy Leary* • **Drunk** *Actors Richard Burton and Elizabeth Taylor in* Who's Afraid of Virginia Woolf • **Duh** *Fatty Arbuckle in* The Sheriff • **Electrocute** *Death penalty advocates in South Carolina* • **Goatee** *Frank Zappa* • **Grapefruit** *Actress Dagmar picking grapefruit* • **G-string** *Stripper Pat Halliday in New Orleans* • **Half-breed** *Cher* • **Hamburger** *McDonald's Museum* • **Hippie** *Hippies doing their thing* • **Hodad** *Nuns catch a wave* • **Holdup** *Patty Hearst in the Symbionese Liberation Army* • **Home run** *Jackie Robinson at home plate, 1947* • **Hula Hoop** *Mimi Jordan, Hula-Hoop Champion* • **Intestinal fortitude** *Eisenhower, Patton, and Truman* • **Jumbo** *Woman with a giant bean from her garden* • **Lasso** *Roy Rogers and Roy Rogers, Jr.* • **Lifestyle** *Halston and an actress with hats* • **Mailman** *Santa's post office helpers* • **Meter maid** *Meter maid at work* • **Moonwalk** *Apollo 12 astronauts on the moon* • **Mossback** *Pat Buchanan* • **Motel** *Deluxe motel bed* • **Motorcade** *Secret Service agents protect President Ronald Reagan* • **Movie** *Orson Welles in* Citizen Kane • **Multicultural** *Sammy Davis Jr. with wife May Britt* • **Mutt** *Tiger riding skateboard* • **Muumuu** *A fan approaches President John Kennedy's car* • **Narc** *Nancy Reagan* • **Necking** *Teenagers doing their thing* • **Nisei** *Japanese-American family sent to an internment camp* • **OK** *Joseph McCarthy* • **Op art** *Op-art shirt* • **Paycheck** *Arnold Palmer waves winnings* • **Pedal pushers** *Jane Powell in pedal pushers action* • **Perfectionism** *The hands of Ben Hogan* • **Phony** *Beatles impersonators* • **Pizza** *Sophia Loren making pizza* • **Play-by-play** *Walter "Red" Barber* • **Poker** *Poker table* • **Popcorn** *Orville Redenbacher* • **Prom** *Liz Taylor at the UCLA prom* • **Quickie** *Couple in train station* • **Rabbit ears** *Juggler Ben Beri* • **Rayon** *Joan Crawford and family* • **Rec room** *Prisoners exercise for synthetic diet experiment* • **Rodeo** *Cowboy riding horse in rodeo* • **Roller coaster** *Corkscrew roller coaster* • **Running mate** *Dan Quayle rally* • **Runway** *Miss Arkansas* • **RV** *The Kangaroo Camper* • **Saguaro** *Campfire beneath a saguaro* • **Salesperson** *Paul Kolenda and his sons* • **Scalawag** *Illustration from 1866 Tuscaloosa newspaper* • **Sex kitten** *Pinup girl Bettie Page* • **Shotgun** *Gary Cooper and Ernest Hemingway* • **Show business** *Ronald Reagan and family* • **Sky marshal** *Passengers or air marshals in disguise* • **Snafu** *The* Hindenburg • **Sneaker** *Paul McCartney* • **Socialite** *Brenda Frazier Kelly Chatfield-Taylor* • **Soul music** *Aretha Franklin* • **Stampede** *Washington, D.C., shoppers* • **Sundae** *Miss Teenage America contestants* • **Tacky** *Harry James and bride* • **Tattletale** *John W. Dean III testifying before the Senate* • **Teenager** *Beatles fans* • **Tepee** *Birch bark tepee* • **Tomahawk** *Indian Brave Grey Eagle* • **Typewriter** *Richard Wright* • **Underpants** *Miniature golf at a tailor's shop* • **Widget** *How to use a remote control* • **Zillion** *Baseball fans*